FACTS AND
FICTION ABOUT
DRUGS™

VAPING

Published in 2020 by The Rosen Publishing Group, Inc.
29 East 21st Street, New York, NY 10010

First Edition

Library of Congress Cataloging-in-Publication Data

Names: McCormick, Anita Louise, author.
Title: Vaping / Anita Louise McCormick.
Description: First edition. | New York : Rosen Publishing, 2020. | Series: Facts and fiction about drugs | Includes bibliographical references and index.
Identifiers: LCCN 2019014363| ISBN 9781725347700 (library bound) | ISBN 9781725347694 (pbk.)
Subjects: LCSH: Vaping—Juvenile literature. | Teenagers—Tobacco use—Juvenile literature.
Classification: LCC HV5748 .M33 2020 | DDC 362.29/6—dc23
LC record available at https://lccn.loc.gov/2019014363

Some of the images in this book illustrate individuals who are models. The depictions do not imply actual situations or events.

Manufactured in the United States of America

CONTENTS

INTRODUCTION

A new drug epidemic is happening in schools.

But this drug epidemic is different. Many teens who become addicted do not even realize they are taking drugs. The epidemic is vaping, and the drug that teens are becoming addicted to is nicotine.

At first, vaping devices, sometimes known as e-cigarettes, were presented as a helpful product. They came on the market as an aid for adult smokers who wanted to quit cigarettes. However, as the popularity of vaping grew, something unexpected happened. Teens who had never smoked decided to try vaping.

When vaping first became popular, many teens asked themselves, "Why not vape?" After all, many of their friends were vaping. Radio, magazine, and internet ads talked about vaping being a safe alternative to smoking. And vaping products came in so many appealing flavors. Sometimes, teens found themselves at a party or a friend's house where different kinds of vaping devices were being passed around. They saw friends doing tricks with vape steam and others applauding.

At first glance, vaping can seem harmless. But is it really?

While vaping is considered somewhat safer than smoking, that does not mean it is safe. Vapers do not inhale tar and other harmful chemicals like smokers, but most of the vaping devices sold in stores contain as much nicotine as cigarettes. And nicotine is extremely addictive.

Vaping devices were originally manufactured as a way to help people stop smoking. However, many teens who have never smoked cigarettes also use vaping devices.

By the time teens realize how much nicotine vaping devices contain, they are often addicted.

The popularity of vaping by teens, especially those who do not smoke cigarettes, soon caused concern in the medical community. In December 2018, the US surgeon general made a statement warning that vaping was now an epidemic among teens. More than 3.6 million teens, including one in five high school students and one in twenty middle school students, reported using e-cigarettes in 2018.

CHAPTER ONE

How Vaping Started

If it was not for addiction to the nicotine in cigarettes, vaping devices would never have been invented. Cigarettes first became popular in the United States in the early twentieth century. Relatively few people smoked cigarettes back then. During World War I and World War II, however, cigarette smoking increased dramatically. This was mostly due to widespread advertising campaigns the tobacco companies ran. The tobacco companies did many things to encourage people to smoke. Their push to promote smoking included radio and newspaper advertising campaigns. Many of the most popular radio programs at the time were sponsored by tobacco companies. Companies that wanted to encourage smoking also gave out free samples of cigarettes to convince people to try them.

Beginning in the 1900s, cigarette companies used advertisements to make cigarettes seem more appealing. After the health effects of smoking became known, governments took steps to restrict advertising.

Tobacco companies were especially interested in targeting people in the military with their marketing campaigns. They sent free packs of cigarettes to soldiers, claiming they were sending cigarettes to help their morale. Tobacco companies also encouraged family and friends to send packs of cigarettes to soldiers as gifts. When soldiers who had taken up smoking in the military returned to civilian life, most continued to smoke.

When cigarette smoking first became popular in the early twentieth century, people had no idea that smoking could cause health problems. They viewed smoking as a harmless pastime. Today, we know that smoking is a very unhealthy thing to do. Medical experts found that smoking can cause lung cancer,

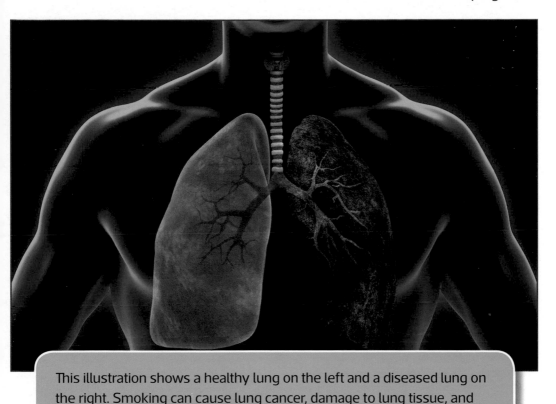

This illustration shows a healthy lung on the left and a diseased lung on the right. Smoking can cause lung cancer, damage to lung tissue, and heart disease.

heart failure, and other diseases. Many of these diseases are caused by smokers inhaling the chemicals contained in smoke from burning tobacco.

Health Concerns

By the 1930s, people were starting to realize that smoking was not a healthy activity. At the time, only a few medical studies had been published about health problems caused by cigarettes. But people were starting to wonder if cigarette smoking was safe.

Some people who smoked cigarettes noticed that smoking made them cough. Others noticed that smoking made it hard

A HISTORY OF VAPING

While vaping is often seen as a modern invention, it actually has a long history. From the time that people began to have health concerns about smoking, inventors have looked for ways to make a smoke-free device that provided nicotine without the health dangers of inhaling smoke.

1930: The first patent for an electronic cigarette is issued to an inventor named Joseph Robinson. However, the device was never manufactured.

1963: A young war veteran named Herbert Gilbert patents an idea for manufacturing an e-cigarette, a device that produces vapor by heating instead of burning tobacco. However, the device was never put on the market.

1964–1999: From the 1960s to the end of the century, tobacco companies occasionally consider the idea of manufacturing devices that deliver nicotine without burning tobacco. A few designs were put on the market, but they did not sell well.

1981: Dr. Norman L. Jacobson first uses the term "vaping" to describe electronic cigarettes. Dr. Jacobson had participated in experimental trials and the production of early vaping devices in the late 1970s.

2004: A Chinese pharmacist, Hon Lik, invents a device that uses electricity to heat a nicotine solution and turn it into a vapor. He files for a patent and puts his product on the market in China. He names his company Ruyan, which means "resembling smoking."

2005–2006: In 2005, Ruyan begins exporting e-cigarettes to Europe. Ruyan begins exporting to the United States in 2006.

2008: E-cigarettes slowly gain popularity, and medical experts begin to take notice. The World Health Organization (WHO) expresses concerns about their safety.

2017: Juul becomes the most popular vaping device in the United States.

to breathe. Yet when smokers tried to stop, they soon realized they were addicted. The chemical they were addicted to was nicotine. Nicotine is in all tobacco products.

During the 1950s, several medical studies concluded that cigarettes caused lung cancer and other serious health problems. The studies also found that the more people smoked, the more likely they were to get sick.

Medical studies concluded that using tobacco in other ways was not healthy either. Smoking tobacco in pipes and chewing tobacco also cause health problems.

When more people became aware of the dangers of smoking, cigarette company executives were worried. They were afraid that smokers would decide to stop smoking and the companies would go out of business.

In hopes of keeping smokers from trying to quit, cigarette companies started to manufacture cigarettes that had filters. These filters were designed to filter out tar. Tar is a name for the toxic chemicals that are released when tobacco is burned. The

Many people who smoke would like to quit. Nicotine gum and patches are designed to help with nicotine withdrawal symptoms.

cigarette companies also created ad campaigns that promoted their products as safe.

During the 1960s, smokers bought more filtered cigarettes than cigarettes that had no filters. Filtered cigarettes removed some tar, but they were still far from being safe.

As time went on, medical experts learned more about ways that smoking can make people ill. This prompted more people who smoked cigarettes to try and quit. However, they soon learned that stopping nicotine use was very difficult.

As a result, aids for people who wanted to quit smoking were developed. These aids gave smokers a way of getting nicotine without the health risks of smoking. They included chewing gum that contained nicotine and nicotine patches. While these aids made quitting easier for some, many smokers were still not able to break their addiction to nicotine.

This led the way for e-cigarettes and other vaping devices to come onto the market.

HOW VAPING WORKS

Most cigarettes look very similar. But vaping devices can look very different. Some vaping devices look very similar to regular cigarettes. They are often called e-cigarettes, or e-cigs. Although some vaping devices are disposable, many kinds can be refilled. Some vaping devices use prefilled cartridges that contain vaping liquid or oil. Other vaping devices are refilled with liquid, called vape juice.

Vaping is still relatively new. Because of this, there is no real standard as to how vaping devices are made and what they look like. No matter what size or shape they are, however, all vaping devices do one thing. They heat the contents of cartridges until they can be inhaled as vapor.

In order to heat the vaping liquid or cartridge, all vaping devices use a battery. This battery is specially made to produce the amount of electricity necessary to produce enough heat to transform vaping liquid or oil into vapor. When people use a vaping device, they breathe in the vapor, which contains nicotine, flavors, and other chemicals.

Some vaping devices are disposable, while others can be recharged. There are even vaping device batteries that can be charged with the USB drive on a computer.

Vaping Becomes Popular

Cigarettes are made from tobacco rolled up tightly in paper. They have to be lit and burn to be smoked. E-cigarettes and other vaping devices operate in a very different way. They are electronic devices that do not burn anything. Instead, they heat liquid, usually containing nicotine, until it is hot enough to produce vapor that users inhale.

For some smokers, vaping devices had distinct advantages over nicotine gum, the patch, and other approaches. That is because vaping devices do not just deliver nicotine. They also give smokers an experience that is more like smoking. For many smokers, using a vaping device feels more like smoking than other methods of nonsmoking nicotine delivery. Vaping devices give smokers something to hold in their hand, to put into their mouth, and also to inhale.

Laws that forbid smokers to light up in businesses, on public transportation, at schools, and many public places made vaping an attractive option for many smokers. This was especially true of heavy smokers who were so addicted to nicotine that they found it very difficult to wait until they were home from school or work to smoke.

As more smokers turned to vaping, new vape companies entered the market. Before long, vaping devices and supplies were for sale almost everywhere that cigarettes were sold. As vaping's popularity grew, many different kinds of vaping devices came on the market. Some looked almost like regular cigarettes, but others looked like computer flash drives. Vape shops also opened in many cities and towns.

There are a wide range of vaping devices on the market today. Most of them look nothing like traditional cigarettes.

Many smokers wanted to kick the cigarette habit, so they decided to try e-cigarettes. For some, the use of vaping devices helped make it possible for them to smoke fewer cigarettes. Some smokers were eventually able to quit altogether and not smoke or vape.

At the same time, a new group of people were starting to buy vaping devices and products: teens who had never smoked before.

CHAPTER TWO

Teens and Vaping

While fewer teens smoke than in the past, vaping is on the rise. According to the Centers for Disease Control and Prevention (CDC), in 2018, more than 3.6 million US middle and high school students had used e-cigarettes within the past thirty days, including 4.9 percent of middle school students and 20.8 percent of high school students.

As with cigarette smoking, teens who vape have many reasons for trying their first e-cigarette. The top three reasons for vaping are because a friend or family member vaped, the appeal of flavored vaping products, and the belief that vaping is safer than smoking.

Flavored Vaping Devices

In 2015, a new company called Juul started making vaping devices. In a growing market, the company wanted to do something to stand out from the competition and bring attention

Juul sells more vaping devices and cartridges than any other company in the industry. Much of their appeal stems from the fact that they sell cartridges in flavors such as cucumber and creme.

to its products. One approach Juul used was to offer flavored vaping cartridges.

By the end of 2017, over 70 percent of people who vaped in the United States were buying Juul. This happened mostly because of the new line of flavored vaping products the company offered.

In addition to regular tobacco cartridges, Juul manufactured cartridges in flavors such as mango, cucumber, mint, and fruit. These flavored cartridges attracted many new customers. They were especially appealing to teens who did not care for the taste of tobacco. Before long, Juul's brand became so popular that people started to refer to vaping as Juuling.

Peer Pressure to Vape

Peer pressure is another reason teens decide to start vaping. Many teens know at least one person who vapes. It might be a close friend or an older brother or sister. It might be a parent who is trying to quit smoking. It could be people in a group or club. Or it might be someone you met at a party.

When others in a group are doing something like vaping, it can be hard to say no. The pressure to vape can be difficult to resist. This is especially true when teens do not understand the health risks of vaping. That is why it is so important for teens to learn about the dangers of vaping before they are pressured to try it. Knowing about the health risks of vaping makes it easier to refuse when someone tells them to give it a try.

Teenagers who don't vape may face peer pressure from those who do. Knowing the dangers of vaping may make it easier to say no if you're asked to join in.

Vaping Tricks

Back in the days before smoking was banned in public places, it was not uncommon to see smokers blowing smoke rings. Some smokers did this to impress their friends. Other smokers just blew smoke rings as a way to pass the time.

Vaping devices do not produce smoke. Instead, they produce steam from heated liquid or oil. Still, some people who vape have found ways to use vape steam to do tricks.

After seeing people do these tricks with vape steam, some teens decide to vape so they can try these tricks themselves. They are lured into vaping by the challenge of learning tricks they can do to impress their friends.

Even in areas where public vaping is prohibited, teens have many ways to watch people doing tricks with vape steam. The internet has videos about vape tricks that viewers of any age can watch. Some vapers have YouTube channels that teach others how to do these tricks. Some vape shops have contests with cash prizes for whoever can do the best tricks with vape steam. While these contests are supposed to be only for adults, ages are not always checked.

In a 2019 article in the *Calgary Herald*, student Kayla Wong described how the idea of doing tricks with vape steam got her addicted to vaping. "I believed I had to do it to fit in and get others to like me," Wong said. "I wanted to try those smoke-ring tricks in videos because they looked cool. At sixteen, I walked into a store and the owner knew I was young, but he still sold a vape to me. I had no idea of the risks and knew nothing about vapes. I got addicted."

EASY TO HIDE

Teens who vape often find that vaping devices are easier to hide than regular cigarettes. Part of the reason they can hide the devices is the design. Some vaping devices look like a metal cigarette. This was especially true of the first wave of vaping devices.

But many vaping devices now look nothing like cigarettes. Some look like computer flash drives. Because many students use flash drives in the normal course of their day, they can easily be hidden in plain sight. Students who vape often put them in their pocket, then go outside or to the restroom during the school day for a nicotine hit.

Some vaping devices have rechargeable batteries that can be charged in a laptop's USB port. They often look a lot like computer flash drives.

Easy to Obtain

Nearly all states have strict laws that do not allow anyone under eighteen to buy cigarettes. Some states do not allow people to buy cigarettes or other tobacco products until they are twenty-one. If store employees are caught selling cigarettes to underage youth, they can get in legal trouble. They are also likely to lose their jobs. Few store employees are willing to take that risk.

When e-cigarettes and other vaping products came on the market, they were not put in the same category as cigarettes. No one knew that teens who did not smoke would want to buy them. This had not happened with other nicotine products that were designed to stop smoking, such as nicotine gum and patches.

Several states, including California, Massachusetts, Virginia, and Utah, have passed laws raising the legal age to buy tobacco products, vaping devices, and vaping supplies to twenty-one.

So, for the most part, when vaping suddenly became popular with teens, few laws were in place to prevent underage teens from buying them.

Laws put in place to prevent underage teens from buying tobacco often did not cover the sale of products intended to help people stop smoking. With no laws stopping them, many teens have been able to buy vaping products at convenience stores and other shops.

When lawmakers realized that underage teens were buying vaping products, they went into action. They pushed for laws that would make it illegal to sell vaping devices or supplies to underage youth. But, by then, many teenagers were already addicted.

Given vaping's popularity, vape shops have opened throughout the country, including this store in Portland, Maine, which sells vaping devices and cartridges.

Undetectable Odor

Everyone knows that burning cigarettes have a strong odor! When people smoke cigarettes, they can't hide it. Even if they go outside to smoke, people can smell the odor of burning cigarettes on their breath and their clothes.

On the other hand, vaping devices, especially those using flavored cartridges, usually have very little telltale odor. The flavors and lack of tobacco odor make vaping difficult to detect. When teachers and parents smell fruit and bubble gum flavors, they usually don't think of nicotine. Instead they think that teen has probably been eating candy or chewing gum. Some schools have rules against students eating candy or chewing gum during class. But the penalties for doing those things are usually much less extreme than for smoking cigarettes or vaping on school property.

DOS AND DON'TS

Do go to medical websites to read about the dangers of vaping.
Don't depend on vape advertisements for information about the dangers of vaping.

Do read the fine print on the device's package to find out if it contains nicotine and how much.
Don't assume that fruit-flavored vaping cartridges contain no nicotine.

Do go to medical websites and read how addictive the nicotine vaping devices contain can be.
Don't let friends or older teens convince you that vaping is not addictive.

Increased Nicotine Consumption

Before vaping, cigarettes were the primary way people took in nicotine. Many years ago, you could see people smoking almost anywhere. Today, there are laws that ban smoking in public places. Smokers are limited in where they can light up. Because of the bans, smokers cannot light up a cigarette at school, at most workplaces, in restaurants, on buses, on aircraft, or in many other places.

But then vaping devices came on the market. Since vaping devices did not smell bad or make smoke, people started vaping in many locations where they were not permitted to smoke.

Because their odor is so hard to detect, teens started vaping in places they would not have been allowed to smoke. One consequence is that teens who vape often take in more nicotine than teens who smoke cigarettes. Once this issue came to the attention of lawmakers, they started taking action.

Health Hazards

In the United States, cigarettes have been around for more than a hundred years. This has given medical experts a lot of time to study the health problems smoking can cause. Vaping is relatively new, so scientists are still learning about the health problems that vaping can cause.

From the time vaping devices came on the market, they were promoted as being less harmful than cigarettes. This is because users were not inhaling smoke and the tar that cigarettes contain. However, the vast majority of vaping products contain nicotine, which is an addictive drug.

Once vaping became popular, a lot of companies started making vaping devices. Many companies, including Juul, started making many kinds of flavored products to use in those devices.

The large number of vaping products now on the market makes it much harder for medical experts to study their risks. Each brand and flavor of vaping product contains different chemicals. It will probably take many years before medical experts will be able to study them all.

In addition to the short-term health problems these chemicals might cause, little is known about the long-term effects of heating them to the high temperatures needed for vaping. The only way to avoid these health risks is not to vape.

Teens and Nicotine

One chemical that is in most vaping products is nicotine. This is a chemical medical experts know is not safe. Nicotine is a very addictive drug. Using vaping products that contain any amount of nicotine exposes people to this addictive drug. Nicotine is particularly harmful to teens because of the way it affects their developing brains.

Some teens do not realize that most flavored vaping products, such as flavored vaping cartridges manufactured by Juul, contain high amounts of nicotine. One Juul vaping cartridge can contain as much nicotine as a pack of cigarettes.

Because nicotine is so addictive, teens sometimes make bad decisions to get the money they need to buy vaping products. For some teens, problems that come from addiction can have very serious impacts on their lives.

In a 2019 NBC News report, Luka Kinard, a fifteen-year-old high school student in High Point, North Carolina, said he knew his vaping habit was out of control because he was spending more than a hundred dollars a week to buy vape refills and doing whatever it took to get the money to feed his habit. During this time, his grades fell and he became upset about things that had not bothered him before. He also lost interest in activities that used to bring him joy.

Then one day, Luka had a seizure and had to be taken to the hospital. Doctors told his parents that vaping was the cause.

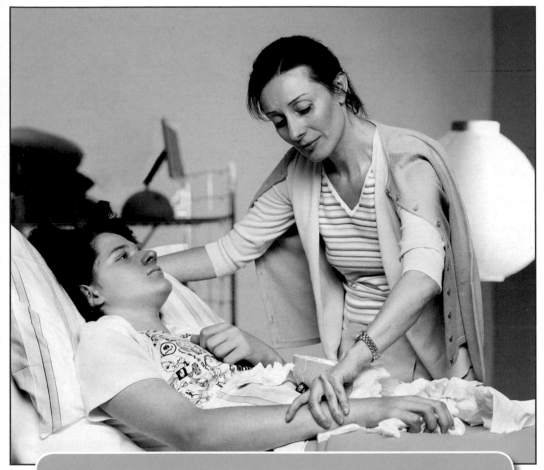

When teens start vaping, they often have no idea about the health, relationship, and behavioral problems that result from becoming addicted to nicotine.

Luka had to spend forty days in an addiction rehab program before he was able to beat his addiction.

Vapers into Smokers

Vaping is still relatively new. But researchers have found that teens who use vaping devices have a higher risk than nonvaping teens to start smoking cigarettes. Medical experts are still trying to understand why this is happening.

Vaping devices that deliver nicotine can be what is called a gateway drug. A gateway drug is something that seems relatively harmless. But using a gateway drug can cause users to be more likely to move on to other drugs. The drugs the gateway drug leads people to try are often much more dangerous.

In this case, taking in nicotine by vaping can lead teens to start smoking. Once they are smoking, they are not only taking in nicotine but are also being affected by the additional health hazards that come from breathing in cigarette smoke.

EXPLODING BATTERIES

Nicotine and other chemicals in vaping cartridges are not the only risks that come with vaping. The batteries used in vaping devices are different from the batteries you use in a flashlight or radio. They are made to heat vaping cartridges or liquids to high temperatures. While it does not happen frequently, the battery that powers vaping devices can explode. When this happens, it often causes severe burns. At least one person has been killed by an exploding vaping device.

In a 2016 NBC News report, "What's Causing Some E-Cigarette Batteries to Explode?," Dr. Anne Wagner of the University of Colorado Hospital (UCH) Burn Center explained what happens when vape batteries explode. Dr. Wagner said, "It's literally an explosion, a super-hot explosion. We're seeing deep third-degree burns and almost all of them require skin grafts and these grafts leave a significant scar."

Vaping Marijuana

Nicotine is not the only drug that people vape. After marijuana became legal for adults to buy and use as a recreational drug in some states, vaping companies saw this as a new market. Many people who smoked cigarettes were now getting nicotine by vaping. So they figured that some marijuana users might want to consume marijuana products without smoking. They started to make vaping cartridges that contain extracts of the marijuana plant.

When marijuana-based vaping products became available, teens started finding ways to obtain them. Vaping marijuana-based products is sometimes known as dabbing.

Some marijuana-based vaping cartridges contain CBD oil. The initials CBD stand for cannabidiol. This is a substance that is found in both marijuana and hemp plants. Hemp plants looks similar to marijuana, but hemp does not contain the chemicals that make people high. Hemp can used to make rope, fabric, paper, and many other products.

Even though some CBD oil comes from marijuana plants, cannabidiol does not make people high. However, some CBD vaping cartridges also contain other chemicals that can cause serious health problems.

An article in *Newsweek* magazine, "Vaping with Fake Pot Leads to Two U.S. Army Deaths and Dozens of Hospitalizations," reported that in January 2018, more than sixty troops stationed in North Carolina became sick after vaping CBD oil and had to be taken to the hospital. They told the doctors they were having headaches, were nauseous, and vomiting. Some had seizures. Medical experts found that the CBD oil the troops vaped contained an artificial chemical. It is called synthetic cannabinoid. These chemicals are sometimes known as fake

CBD oil and had seizures and died from falls or accidents. After that happened, the Army Public Health Center published a statement warning against vaping CBD oil.

A Dangerous High

Some marijuana users use vape cartridges that contain tetrahydrocannabinol (THC). THC is the chemical in marijuana

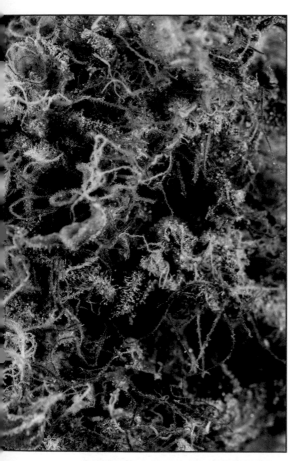

that makes people high. THC is also used in medical marijuana products that are legal to use and sell in some states. Some marijuana vaping devices can be filled with marijuana leaves or buds. Other marijuana devices use oils or liquids that contain THC.

When people vape marijuana, they avoid some of the health issues that can be caused by smoking. However, most people who vape THC have no idea how much they are consuming. Many vaping products deliver a high concentration of THC. This amount is a higher level of THC than most medical marijuana products or marijuana people smoke as recreational users.

When people use marijuana in a vaping device, the high levels of THC can make them very intoxicated. They may feel physically sick, anxious, or even experience hallucinations.

This can cause people who vape THC products to become very intoxicated. In some cases, it has also led to mental health issues.

In a December 2018 article in *Science Daily*, Ryan Vandrey, associate professor of psychiatry and behavioral sciences at the Johns Hopkins University School of Medicine said:

> What our study suggests is that some people who use cannabis infrequently need to be careful about how much cannabis they use with a vaporizer, and they should not drive, even within several hours after use. It could be dangerous for themselves and others, and on top of that, they may experience negative effects such as anxiety, nausea, vomiting, and even hallucinations.

Other Vaping Ingredients

Following the popularity of Juul's flavored vaping cartridges, more companies decided to manufacture vaping devices that deliver caffeine and flavors, instead of nicotine. Some vaping websites have forums where people write about unusual things they tried to vape. These things include catnip, cooking herbs, and other substances.

People who vape these substances have no idea how safe they are. No one knows how much harm these products might cause when they are vaped. Medical experts are concerned about the long-term effects. Sometimes, things that are safe to eat can be dangerous when heated to high temperatures and inhaled.

Dangers of Nicotine

Every day, most of us see people smoking, vaping, or using other products that contain nicotine. Because nicotine use is

It is difficult to break an addiction to nicotine and the withdrawal symptoms, such as headaches and nausea, can be hard to bear. But if you can stay away from nicotine, the symptoms do get better.

so widespread, it can be easy to think that nicotine use is not as serious a problem as addiction to other drugs. But this is not true. Once a person becomes addicted to nicotine, it can be as hard to quit as stopping heroin use.

Nicotine affects the human brain. A teen's brain is still in the process of developing. This makes teens more sensitive to drugs such as nicotine than adults.

If people who smoke or vape decide to stop, they often have withdrawal symptoms because of their addiction to nicotine.

Some symptoms cigarette smokers and vape users experience when they stop using nicotine are intense cravings for nicotine, headaches, nausea, cramps, sweating, and tingling in the hands and feet. Withdrawal symptoms are often so strong and unpleasant that people go back to using nicotine. But if they are able to endure the withdrawal symptoms, they eventually go away.

CHAPTER FOUR

Slowing the Vaping Epidemic

T oday, efforts to slow the vaping epidemic are in full force. But concerns about the health effects of vaping are not new. From the time vaping devices first came to North America, medical experts had concerns about their safety.

In 2008, when vaping devices were first introduced as the new stop-smoking aid, the Food and Drug Administration (FDA) released a statement that e-cigarettes were unapproved medical devices. That means that they had not been tested for safety or effectiveness. In the years that followed, the FDA released statements about the dangerous ingredients some vaping products contained. The FDA also suggested that vaping devices and products should be regulated like tobacco.

The Canadian Public Health Association has also been working to slow the vaping epidemic. It suggested that the

Canadian government regulate vaping devices and products the same way as tobacco. It also wants the Canadian government to limit the production of vaping flavors that appeal to children and teens and do more research on the safety of chemicals used in vaping products.

Finding Ways to Slow Vaping's Growth

When the vaping epidemic started, lawmakers, schools, and parents were unprepared. No one expected a device that was made to help adult smokers quit would gain such popularity with teens. Especially teens who did not smoke. Because so little information was available, most teens had no idea of the impact vaping could have on their health.

Once medical experts realized they were dealing with a teen vaping epidemic, they started making plans to reverse this dangerous trend.

Many medical experts and lawmakers would like to see flavored vaping products taken off the market, as the availability of so many enticing flavors is what attracts many teens and other first-time users to vaping. Some lawmakers and medical experts would like to see vaping devices sold only to people who are over twenty-one.

In a 2018 interview with NBC News, "Vaping, Juuling Are the New Smoking for High School Kids," FDA commissioner Dr. Scott Gottlieb said, "We're going to hold industry participants responsible for actions that promote youth addiction. There's no acceptable number of children using tobacco products."

In the future, the government is likely to continue passing regulations to help control the youth vaping epidemic. In March 2019, Joe Grogan, director of the White House Domestic Policy Council, told Bloomberg, "Everybody agrees that there's going to be more regulation in the tobacco space. We are extremely concerned about the public health consequences of vaping and e-cigarette use in kids."

Banning Vaping at School

During the school year, teens spend much of their time at school. So banning vaping is one ways schools are attempting to slow the vaping epidemic.

Vaping is now being banned on school property in many areas. If students are caught vaping, they face the same punishment as students who are caught smoking. Officials hope that regulations against vaping on school property will encourage students not to start. They also hope that students who already vape will stop or cut down on vaping. Some schools have installed devices that detect vapors that come from vaping in restrooms.

Unfortunately, many students do not realize how addicted they are to vaping. They only realize how bad their addiction to nicotine is when they have to stop vaping or risk punishment.

In a *New York Times* article, "'I Can't Stop': Schools Struggle with Vaping Explosion," reporter Kate Zernike spoke with Nate Carpenter, the vice principal at Cape Elizabeth High School in Maine. Carpenter had been at the school for four years. Smoking had never been a problem at the school. But within a short time, vaping seemed to be happening everywhere.

One day, a student who had been caught vaping on school property three times was sent to Carpenter's office. When Carpenter asked why the student continued to vape, the answer was simply, "I can't stop."

Some localities are passing laws against vaping in areas where smoking is prohibited. In 2009, Suffolk County, New York,

As more cities and towns ban vaping in public areas, people with nicotine addictions may find that they have fewer and fewer places to legally vape.

became the first municipality in the United States to ban e-cigarette use indoors. As time goes on, many more areas are likely to ban vaping everywhere smoking is banned.

Saying No to Vaping Shops

Another way some communities are dealing with teen vaping is not allowing vape shops to open. In some communities, vape shops are not allowed to operate close to schools. Community leaders realize that if vape shops are not near schools, students are less likely to vape.

Some community leaders have found other ways to fight against the vaping epidemic. They charge high license fees to people who want to open vape shops. Other areas put high taxes on vape shops.

An article in the *Philadelphia Inquirer*, "Vape Tax Brings in Millions—And Is Said to Close Over 100 PA. Businesses,"

RELIABLE RESOURCES

If you or someone you know is trying to stop vaping, it can sometimes be difficult to find dependable information. The organizations listed below offer information and resources on quitting that you can trust.

- **Addiction Education Society:** (650) 445-7464, https://addictioneducationsociety.org: This organization provides information on vaping and other addictions. It has a special section for teen addiction issues. The website includes a directory of organizations that specialize in helping with various kinds of addictions.
- **American Lung Association:** (800) 586-4872, http://www.lung.org: This organization offers information and a free hotline to help people who want to stop smoking or vaping.
- **Partnership for Drug-Free Kids:** (855) 378-4373, https://drugfree.org: This group provides a free helpline and resources about vaping, smoking, and other drug addictions.
- **SmokeFreeTeen:** https://teen.smokefree.gov: This government-run website offers free services to teens who want to stop smoking or vaping. Free services include an app and text messages to help teens quit.

revealed the success of this approach. In 2016, Pennsylvania put a 40 percent tax on vape shops that operated in the state. Within the first year of the new tax, more than one hundred of Pennsylvania's four hundred vape shops closed. The vape shops that stayed open had to charge higher prices. With vaping products costing more, teens were less likely to buy them.

While these approaches have limited teens' access to vaping supplies, it has not solved the problem completely. Once teens become addicted to vaping, they are likely to go out of their way to obtain vaping supplies.

How to Get Help Quitting

If someone you know is vaping and wants to stop, help is available. Deciding to stop vaping and get off nicotine is the first step to success. Kicking the nicotine habit is never easy, but many people have done it. Even people who were addicted to nicotine for decades have quit.

There are many ways to help someone who is addicted to nicotine. One thing you can do is help them find resources. There are many websites that give tips for breaking an addiction to nicotine. Most organizations that work to help people stop smoking also offer suggestions to help people stop vaping.

Vaping is so new that medical experts do not have specific guidelines on how to stop vaping. Many people who quit vaping use the same methods people use to stop smoking cigarettes. These methods include nicotine gum and patches. While these stop-smoking aids still contain nicotine, they can help people gradually step down the amount of nicotine they use. This helps people quit without having as many withdrawal symptoms.

If someone you know wants to stop vaping, you might also suggest that the person talk with parents, teachers, or a doctor about the decision to quit. If there is a nurse at school, he or she might have suggestions as well.

One new way to help teens quit vaping is texting. A nonprofit antismoking organization called Truth Initiative has started a free program that people can enroll in to receive texts to help them quit vaping.

Another great way to help a friend quit vaping is by offering encouragement. Even if people are not successful the first time, they can always try again. Many people who quit smoking did not succeed the first time. But through repeated attempts, they finally were able to quit.

Trying to break an addiction to any drug is not fun. Once people succeed, however, they will tell you it was well worth the effort. Breaking free of an addiction is an accomplishment to be proud of!

Educating the Public About Vaping

While medical and legal experts are debating how to deal with the vaping epidemic, health organizations, government agencies, nonprofit groups, and schools are looking for ways to educate teens about the dangers of vaping. They hope to reach teens with this important information before they start vaping.

This education is being done in many different ways. Many groups that help people stop smoking have become involved. They developed programs schools can use to teach young people about the dangers of vaping. They also have information online that teens, schools, and parents can use to learn more about the dangers of vaping. The more teens know about vaping, the less likely they are to start. And if they don't start, they never have to quit.

ADDICTIVE Likely to cause a person to compulsively use a substance, even though it is harmful.

ALTERNATIVE Another available choice or possibility.

APPROACH A way or method of doing something.

BAN To forbid or make illegal.

CAFFEINE A drug found in coffee, tea, cola, and other drinks that causes people to stay alert.

E-CIGARETTE An electronic device used to deliver nicotine.

ENDURE To put up with; survive through.

EPIDEMIC The spread of an infectious disease or health concern, such as vaping.

HEROIN A highly addictive and dangerous drug made from morphine.

INHALE To breathe something in.

JUULING Another term for vaping, based on a popular brand.

NICOTINE An addictive drug found in tobacco.

REGULATIONS Rules or laws made by a government or other authority.

TAR A toxic byproduct of burning tobacco.

TOXIC Describing a substance that is poisonous.

VAPING Inhaling and exhaling vapor from a vaping product.

VAPOR Gas that is released when a substance is heated.

WITHDRAWAL The symptoms people experience when they stop taking an addictive drug.

Child Mind Institute
101 East 56th Street
New York, NY 10022
(212) 308-3118
Website: https://childmind.org
Facebook: @ChildMindInstitute
Twitter: @ChildMindInst
The Child Mind Institute is a nonprofit independent organization that helps families that have children and teens with learning and mental health issues find help. They offer information on helping teens with addictions to nicotine and other drugs.

Government of Canada
Health Canada
Address Locator 0900C2
Ottawa, Ontario
K1A 0K9
Email: Info@hc-sc.gc.ca
Telephone: (613) 957-2991
Website: https://www.canada.ca/en/health-canada/services/smoking -tobacco.html
The government of Canada offers information to help people quit smoking and vaping. It also offers links to local resources across Canada.

Make Smoking History
250 Washington Street
Boston, MA 02108
(800) QUIT-NOW

Website: http://www.makesmokinghistory.org
Facebook: @MakeSmokingHistory
Twitter: @MakeSmkngHistry
Make Smoking History is a project of the Massachusetts Tobacco
    Cessation and Prevention Program. It provides educational
    resources to help people stop smoking and vaping.

Physicians for a Smoke-Free Canada
134 Caroline Avenue
Ottawa, ON K1Y 0S9
Canada
(613) 297-3590
Website: http://www.smoke-free.ca
Physicians for a Smoke-Free Canada is a national health organization.
    It works to educate the public about the dangers of tobacco use
    and thereby decrease tobacco-caused health problems.

Smokefree
Website: https://teen.smokefree.gov
Facebook: @SmokefreeUS
Twitter: @SmokefreeUs
Smokefree is an organization created by the National Cancer
    Institute. It offers plans, tools and tips, and an app to help
    people stop smoking.

Cornell, Kari A. *E-Cigarettes and Their Dangers* (Drugs and Their Dangers). San Diego, CA: BrightPoint Press, 2019.

Gordon, Sherri Mabry. *Everything You Need to Know About Smoking, Vaping, and Your Health* (The Need to Know Library). New York, NY: Rosen Publishing, 2019.

Hamilton, Tracy Brown. *I Am Addicted to Drugs. Now What?* (Teen Life 411). New York, NY: Rosen Publishing, 2017.

Heing, Bridey. *Marijuana Abuse* (Overcoming Addiction). New York, NY: Rosen Publishing, 2019.

Horning, Nicole. *Drug Addiction and Substance Use Disorders* (Diseases and Disorders). New York, NY: Lucent Books, 2019.

Gordon, Sherri Mabry. *Everything You Need to Know About Smoking, Vaping, and Your Health* (The Need to Know Library). New York, NY: Rosen Publishing, 2019.

Karpan, Andrew. *Vaping* (At Issue). New York, NY: Greenhaven Publishing, 2019.

Krajnik, Elizabeth. *Why Is Smoking Bad for Me?* New York, NY: Rosen Publishing, 2019.

Parks, Peggy J. *The Dangers of E-Cigarettes* (Drug Dangers). San Diego, CA: ReferencePoint Press Inc., 2017.

Snyder, Gail. *Teens and Smoking* (Teen Choices). San Diego, CA: ReferencePoint Press Inc., 2015.

BIBLIOGRAPHY

Calgary Herald. "U of C Group Urges Quick Action to Stop Youths from Vaping." February 23, 2019. https://calgaryherald.com /opinion/columnists/opinion-u-of-c-group-urges-quick-action -to-stop-youths-from-vaping.

Delzo, Janissa. "Vaping with Fake Pot Has Led to Two U.S. Army Deaths and Dozens of Hospitalizations." *Newsweek,* February 1, 2018. https://www.newsweek.com /vaping-fake-pot-army-deaths-hospitalizations-797630.

Fox, Maggie. "Vaping, Juuling Are the New Smoking for High School Kids." NBC News. Retrieved March 14, 2019. https://www .nbcnews.com/health/health-news /vaping-juuling-are-new-smoking-high-school-kids-n881121.

Gebel, Meira. "Vaping Among Teens Skyrocketed in the Last Year as Cigarette Use Declined, New CDC Study Shows." *Business Insider.* Retrieved February 20, 2019. https://www .businessinsider.com/teens-vaping-more-and-smoking-fewer -cigarettes-cdc-study-2019-2.

Hoffman, Jan. "How to Help Teenagers Quit Vaping." *New York Times*, December 18, 2018. https://www.nytimes.com /2018/12/18/health/vaping-teens-nicotine.html.

Lam, Kristin. "FDA Proposes E-Cigarette Sale Restrictions to Curb Teen Vaping." *USA Today.* Retrieved March 14, 2019. https:// www.usatoday.com/story/news/nation/2019/03/13/fda-restricts -e-cigarette-sales-curb-teen-vaping/3157826002.

Martinelli, Katherine. "Teen Vaping: What You Need to Know." Child Mind Institute. Retrieved March 14, 2019. https://childmind .org/article/teen-vaping-what-you-need-to-know.

McDaniel, Justine. "Vape tax brings in millions — and is said to close over 100 Pa. businesses." *Philadelphia Inquirer.* Retrieved March 14, 2019. https://www.inquirer.com/philly/news/pennsylvania/ vape-tax-brings-in-millions-and-closes-over-100-pa- businesses-20170905.html

O'Donnell, Jayne. "FDA Surprise: Commissioner Scott Gottlieb, Aggressive Regulator Against Vaping, Resigns." *USA Today*. Retrieved March 14, 2019. https://www.usatoday.com/story /news/health/2019/03/05/fda-commissioner-scott-gottlieb -resigns-food-drug-administration/3069901002.

Perone, Matthew. "US Health Officials Move to Tighten Sales of E-Cigarettes." The Associated Press, March 13, 2019. https:// www.apnews.com/4276c948366f4879b58aa7ecf2d2451e.

ScienceDaily. "Vaping Cannabis Produces Stronger Effects than Smoking Cannabis for Infrequent Users." Retrieved March 14, 2019. https://www.sciencedaily.com/releases/2018/12 /181204131115.htm.

Smokefree.gov "Nicotine & Addiction | Smokefree Teen." Retrieved March 14, 2019. https://teen.smokefree.gov/the-risks-of -tobacco/nicotine-addiction.

Talev, Margaret, and Anna Edney. "No Letup Seen in Crackdown on Vaping by FDA After Gottlieb." Bloomberg, March 8, 2019. https://www.bloomberg.com/news/articles/2019-03-07/white -house-says-no-dispute-with-fda-chief-gottlieb-before-exit.

Truth Initiative. "Young JUUL Users Now Have a Free Resource to Help Them Quit." Truth Initiative, January 17, 2019. https:// www.truthinitiative.org/news/first-its-kind-free-e-cigarette-quit -program-now-available-young-vapers-looking-help.

Weisbaum, Herb. "What's Causing Some E-Cigarette Batteries to Explode?" NBC News. Retrieved March 14, 2019. https://www .nbcnews.com/business/consumer/what-s-causing-some -e-cigarette-batteries-explode-n533516.

Zernike, Kate. "'I Can't Stop': Schools Struggle with Vaping Explosion." *New York Times*, April 2, 2018. https://www .nytimes.com/2018/04/02/health/vaping-ecigarettes -addiction-teen.html.

INDEX

About the Author

Anita Louise McCormick is the author of many books. Her previous titles for Rosen Publishing include *Tyler Oakley: LGBTQ+ Activist with More Than 660 Million Views*, *Rosa Parks and the Montgomery Bus Boycott*, *The Native American Struggle in United States History*, and *Everything You Need to Know About Nonbinary Gender Identities*.

Photo Credits